TEAM AWE

WIDE RULED COMPOSITION NOTEBOOK

This book belongs to:

Made in the USA
Las Vegas, NV
13 January 2021

15817935R00063